1. Bristol Harbour c.1880, looking towards the old drawbridge. St. Augustine's Parade on the left, and over to the right the tower of St. Stephen's Church, which dates from the 13th century. It was extensively refurbished in 1470. The shops to the right along Broad Quay include ships chandlers, sail makers and nautical instrument manufacturers.

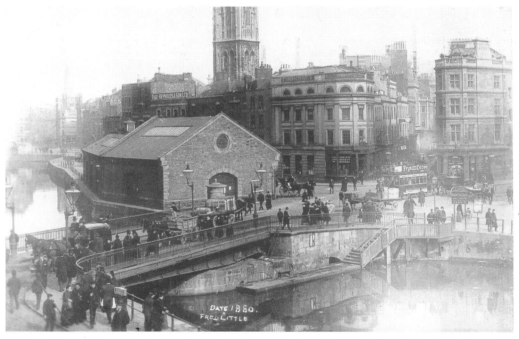

2. The old Drawbridge built in 1868. This was replaced by a wider fixed bridge in 1892-93, when the River Froom, to the left of the Shed, was covered over to form Colston Avenue (Magpie Park). The Shed was built in 1879. The circular building in front of it was a watch box for the police.

3. The Tramway Centre looking towards the bottom of Colston Street. In the centre is Colston Hall, built on the site of the Carmelite priory. Bristol Tramway and Carriage Company Offices are under the clock. These premises were also the offices of Blue Taxis, first registered in 1908 and in business until 1930. Postcard postally used in 1914.

4. The Tramway Centre. A busy scene taken from the bottom of College Green. Shops on the left include R.T. Plum, Cutlers; Dunscombe's; and Husbands, opticians. Beyond the cart in the centre St. Augustines Bridge spans the River Froom which enters here into the Floating Harbour. Tram no. 178 climbs the curve from the Centre towards College Green and Hotwells.

5. Broad Quay taken from the top deck of a tram c.1908 showing the newly-built C.W.S. building at the end of the quay. Close by is the Dublin Shed where ships from Ireland discharged their cargo.

6. The Tramway Centre with several trams awaiting passengers. Adverts for Fry's Chocolate, and Jacobs Cream Crackers are prominent on the side of the trams. Beyond in St. Augustine's Parade is the Bristol Hippodrome, which opened in 1912. The globe on the roof still in place in this picture, was removed in 1964. This view c.1933.

7. Rupert and Quay Streets c.1920's. The building extending into Quay Street is part of J.S. Fry's Chocolate factory. The figurehead on Demerara House came from the S.S. Demerara, the ship broke her back while sailing down the River Avon on her maiden voyage in 1851. Sadly the figurehead disintegrated when the building was demolished prior to the erection of Electricity House in 1939, now used as offices.

8. The fountain in Colston Avenue. Through the trees on the left is the Roman Catholic church of St. Mary's on the Quay built in 1843 and designed by Richard Shackleton Pope. Beyond the lamp standard the statue of Edward Colston erected in 1895, he was founder of Colston School. Postcard postally used in 1913.

9. College Green with the replica High Cross (the original is at Stourhead in Wiltshire). This winter scene gives an impressive view of Bristol Cathedral through the trees. The Cathedral originally St. Augustines Abbey, dates from 1140. It has had extensive alterations over the years, the west towers were completed in 1887.

10. The bottom of Park Street from College Green. On the right the Lord Mayor's Chapel, St. Marks, which dates from 1320, the tower from 1487 and the east end of the church about 1520, with the north transcript a late Victorian rebuild. Postcard postally used in 1910.

11. Cabot Tower built on Brandon Hill, to celebrate the 400th anniversary of the sailing of John Cabot, who discovered Newfoundland in 1497. The tower with cannons around its base, was designed by W.V. Gough. The Marquis of Dufferin and Ava laid the foundation stone in 1897, and the tower opened in 1898.

12. St. Augustine's Church was founded in 1240, and rebuilt in 1480, lengthened in 1780, with further restoration in the 1880's. The church became redundant in the 1930's. It was damaged in an air raid in the last war, and demolished in 1962. The trees in the centre are in College Green and Cabot Tower can be seen in the distance.

13. Park Street looking towards College Green, this view c.1905. A bustling shopping area, many shops with their blinds down. The shops have modern frontage today but the upper windows retain their Georgian architecture, many were rebuilt after war damage.

14. Park Street in the late 1920's, motor vehicles in evidence and the Bristol University Tower newly built. It was completed in 1925.

15. Park Row, towards Queens Road and the top of Park Street with the Coliseum Cinema, which didn't survive when talking films arrived. During the years before 1914, the building was used as a dance hall and ice rink, and in the 1914-18 war Parnell's built aircraft there. Today a newly built department of Bristol University has been built on the site.

16. Perry Road which continues from Park Row. Tram no.9 en route for the Tramway Centre via Whiteladies Road. from Durdham Downs. The terraced houses are in Lower Park Road, and connect with Colston Street. Postcard postally used in 1907.

17. The Princes' Theatre in Park Row c.1910, facing Woodland Road, was built in 1867 and was known locally as the "New Theatre". The theatre was destroyed in air raids in the last war, and never rebuilt.

18. The interior of the Princes Theatre from the stage, showing the fine seating arrangements from the stalls to the gallery. In the gallery the front row was separate with a high wooden back. The decorated boxes either side of the stage complete the auditorium.

19. A procession of discharged soldiers and sailors wending their way from Upper Maudlin Street into Perry Road, passing the turning for Colston Street. It appears to be a protest at their discharge and the lack of employment on leaving the forces. Many banners convey their dissatisfaction.

20. The funeral procession of the late Joseph Storrs Fry, on July 12th 1913. He was the founder of Fry's Chocolate and Cocoa factory. The cortége is wending its way down Upper Maudlin Street and is attracting interest from many onlookers.

21. Bristol Royal Infirmary in Marlborough Street, founded in 1736, with the first patients admitted in 1737. Tram no.15 is wending its way from Durdham Downs down into Lower Maudlin Street en route for Eastville. The building on the left with the rounded roof is part of the new B.R.I. building which was built as a memorial to Edward VII and opened by King George V in 1912.

22. The nurses home for the staff of Bristol Royal Infirmary, viewed from the Edward VII memorial hospital of 1912. Many of the houses beyond are in Kingsdown. On the extreme right the tower of H.H. Wills physics laboratory and Royal Fort; a department of Bristol University.

23. Christmas Steps from the corner with Host Street and Lewin's Mead, a narrow alley with many steps up into Colston Street, c.1910. At the top on an adjoining wall of John Fosters Almshouses is an inscription, "This street was steppered, done and finished September 1669".

24. Broad Street, a cobbled small road off of Corn Street, c.1910. St. John's Church, with three arches, is the only surviving gate of the old city wall.

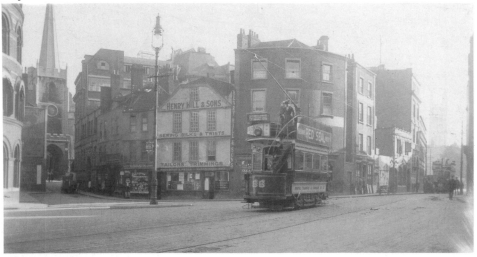

25. Rupert Street with tram no.66 en route for Horfield Barracks, passing Christmas Street. This is the other side of St. John's Church and arches (picture 24) all the properties on the right in Christmas Street were later pulled down and Electricity House was built on the site in 1938-39.

26. The Horsefair c.1912. Through the trees of St. James Park, the square tower of St. James Church. Further along is St. James Presbyterian Church built in 1859, this later became the Welsh Congregational Church. It was burnt out on 24th November 1940, and the spire removed in the 1950's. A group of people pose for the photographer around the cabman's hut.

27. The Horsefair in 1880. The fair was held annually on this site from the Middle Ages, and it was originally part of St. James Churchyard. This view shows the Golden Gallopers just waiting for its riders! Lewis's a modern department store was built here in the 1950's. It was taken over in recent years by John Lewis. There is a proposed new owner for the store in the coming year.

28. The Upper Arcade between the Horsefair and St. James Barton. The site is marked today as a walkway with steps, between John Lewis and Debenhams Stores. Built in 1825, it was destroyed in an air raid, on November 24th 1940.

29. The Lower Arcade built at the same time as the upper one in 1825. It was designed by James Foster, assistant of William Paty. This view shows the entrance from Broadmead, and survives today restored to its original design. The steps have been replaced by a sloping walkway.

CENTRAL BRISTOL

30. This view from half-way down Union Street, looking towards the Horsefair in 1926. The shops on the left include Ferris & Co., chemists, and further down on the same side the premises of J.S. Fry and Sons Ltd., cocoa and chocolate manufacturers. The right hand side was completely rebuilt in the 1950's.

31. Lower Union Street in the 1920's. The building behind the policeman is Strode, Cosh and Penford, chemists. Their shop extended into Broadmead. On the same side is Broadmead Baptist Chapel. The congregation of Baptists was founded in 1640. The historic chapel constructed in 1695, was rebuilt and enlarged in 1877. The present modern chapel was designed by Ronald Sims, 1967-69.

32. Broadmead in the early 1900's. A cart in the loading bay of J.S. Fry's Chocolate Factory, and a horse and loaded cart nearby. Fry's factory moved to Somerdale at Keynsham in 1924-25. Today the site is shared by the Odeon cinema and a Mothercare shop.

33. John Wesley's first chapel built in 1739, which he called the "New Room". It was enlarged in 1740's. Wesley first preached Methodism in the open air to miners and local people in the Kingswood area, and he opened a school there. This postcard shows a service being held to commemorate the renovation and re-opening of the chapel in February 1930.

34. Newfoundland Street in the 1920's. When this picture was taken the street connected with Milk Street and the Horsefair, today it joins the ring road in Bond Street. This bustling view looking towards Newfoundland Road. The one surviving building on the left is the Magnet Cinema, used as offices today.

MAGNET CINEMA THEATRE, Newfoundland Street, St. Paul's, BRISTOL.

35. The Magnet Cinema, c.1910, showing its distinctive arch doorway, and two rounded windows either side of the centre window above. The film showing "England Expects", two shows nightly 6-45 and 8-45 p.m. and seats at 2p, 3p, 4p and 6p! The dearest seats 2$\frac{1}{2}$p in today's money! Next door is Wensley's general draper.

36. Old Market Street c.1930's with many trams at the terminus, their prominent poles and connecting wires in the middle of the road. Further down on the right the round tower of the Central Hall, which opened in April 1924. J. Arthur Rank (later Lord Rank) donated £25,000 towards its cost.

37. Old Market Street c.1914. The Empire Theatre opened in 1893 with twice nightly shows. It specialised in Music Hall and Variety acts. Tram no. 180 is en route for St. George and Kingswood. The light building on the right of the picture, the Stag and Hounds one of the few buildings surviving today.

38. Old Market Street. Another picture of the street in the same period as illustration 37. This view looks along the opposite side of the street. On the right W.J. Rogers Ltd., brewers, their offices and brewery extend into Broad Plain. Further along beyond the four trams another view of the Stag and Hounds Inn.

39. Tower Hill looking up towards Old Market Street, in 1924, shows a flourishing thoroughfare. On the left a Shellfish and Oyster Bar, and opposite the Prince of Wales Inn, specialising in Rogers prize medal ales. Tram 198 about to descend.

40. Castle Street c.1916. A busy shopping area, a barrow boy with his white coat, selling fresh fruit and vegetables. The street connected with Old Market and extends to Peter Street.

41. Castle Street in December 1936. Christmas shoppers outside British Home Stores, advertising goods from 3 pence (1$\frac{1}{2}$p) to 5 shillings (25p).

42. Peter Street, a turning off of Dolphin Street, which joins on the left with Little Peter Street and on the right Castle Street. These streets were the centre of the shopping area before the last war, and were largely destroyed in an air raid in 1940. The whole area around these few streets now an open space, Castle Park.

43. Little Peter Street. On the right the "Bear and Rugged Staff". One of Bristol's earliest inns, built in 1653. The name taken from the armorial bearings of the house of Warwick. Further down on the corner with Castle Green, the "Cat and Wheel", which existed before 1606, originally known as "The Catherine Wheel". This view shows the inn rebuilt in 1901.

44. Ellbroad Street on a busy day in the early 1900's. Pigs being driven to be slaughtered, and a loaded cart waiting to pass through. The road connects Redcross Street with Broad Weir.

45. Narrow Wine Street continues from Wine Street, a quaint street, no longer existing today.

46. Wine Street c.1912 from the top of Union Street. The Don specialising in boys clothes on the left, and on the other side shops include, England & Sons domestic bazaar. The spire of Christ Church can be seen, famous for its striking clock and quarter jacks, dating from 1740.

47. The Corn Exchange in Corn Street. The Exchange designed by John Wood 1741-43. The "Nails" standing in the front of the building a gift of wealthy merchants, used for business deals to be settled. Hence the quote "Paying on the Nail".

48. The Flower Market adjoining Nicholas Street, built in 1745. Flower girls sitting on boxes ready to sell their blooms, an advertisement for Diadem Flour on the archway which leads into the High Street. Postcard postally used in 1905.

49. Corn Street from the corner with St. Stephens Street, one of the main centres of banking in the city. Further up the street All Saints Church, dating from the Norman period, with later extensions in the 15th century. The tower, however, early Georgian. The church contains a monument to Edward Colston, merchant, and founder of Colston School.

50. Clare Street from the Tramway Centre. Further up it joins Corn Street. The street is also a centre for banking and insurance offices. On the left is the London & Lancashire Assurance Company. The postcard postally used in 1908.

51. Broad Street in the 1920's looking towards St. John the Baptist Church and the three arches. The narrow lanes either side of the church are Bell Lane, and Tower Lane. The Guildhall on the left is early Victorian, it opened in 1846 on the site of a much earlier building.

52. Small Street in the 1920's, early motor cars and delivery vans parked. The quaint half timbered shop owned by C.J. Hill sold shirts and other menswear. Further down on the left the General Post Office, although not in view.

53. Mary-le-Port Street in the 1920's, but the card not posted until 1937. A narrow street with gabled houses and shops, it joins into High Street. The roof of the Flower Market at the far end.

54. All Saints Lane from Corn Street. Behind the hanging lamp the iron spars of the roof of the Flower Market, and the spire of St. Nicholas Church beyond. By the lamp the Rummer Hotel. This view c.1908.

55. The Dutch House on the corner of High Street and Wine Street, dates from 1676. This crossroad was the site of the original medieval High Cross c.1373. Advertisements on the shops on the left include H. Samuel - lucky wedding rings, and Salmon and Gluckstein Ltd., while on the Dutch House in the High Street is MacDonalds Teeth - Dental Consulting Rooms; Barlock Typewiters and Olivers Advertising Agency, with the Great Western Railways general enquiries and receiving office next door.

56. The Pithay c.1880. The sign above the two women and child, Christ Church Mission, and opposite T.J. Gardner Plane and Toolmaking Manufacturers, the smaller sign Good Lodging for travellers. Today the Pithay connects with Fairfax Street and Wine Street, and only the name survives. The Pithay was formerly known as Aylward Street after the Alwards a once great local family. Nearly all the old dwellings here were pulled down in 1898 to provide a site for an extension of the chocolate and cocoa manufacturers Messrs. Fry and Sons.

57. Castle Green c.1900, between Castle Street and Tower Lane. The buildings on the right built on the site of the old Bristol Castle. A small girl with a wide brimmed hat poses for the photographer.

58. Dolphin Street which connected Bridge Street and Union Street. The street decorated to celebrate the opening of the Royal Edward dock at Avonmouth, by Edward VII and Queen Alexandra, on July 8th 1908.

59. Bridge Street wending its way up to the left, at the top the tower of St. Peters' Church. To the right of the City Boot Stores, Bristol Bridge and the river Avon. Georges Brewery can be seen to the right of the picture, established in the 17th century.

60. The High Street from Bristol Bridge, St. Nicholas Church on the left, and on the opposite corner of High Street, the Scholastic Wholesale and Retail Stationers. A prominent view of Christ Church at the top c.1920's.

61. Bristol Bridge looking across to Victoria Street. In the building with the dome are the offices of E.S. & A. Robinson, paper and cardboard manufacturers. The statue is of Samuel Morley, Liberal M.P. for Bristol between 1868-1885, sculpted by J. Havard Thomas, and erected in 1887.

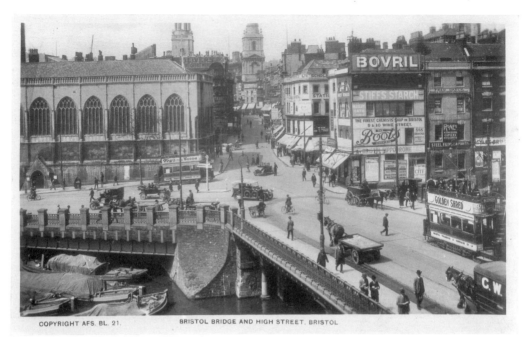

COPYRIGHT AFS. BL. 21.   BRISTOL BRIDGE AND HIGH STREET, BRISTOL

62. Bristol Bridge from the opposite direction c.1931. St. Nicholas Church to the left. Samuel Morley's statue was removed to the Horsefair in 1921, and a signpost installed in its place.

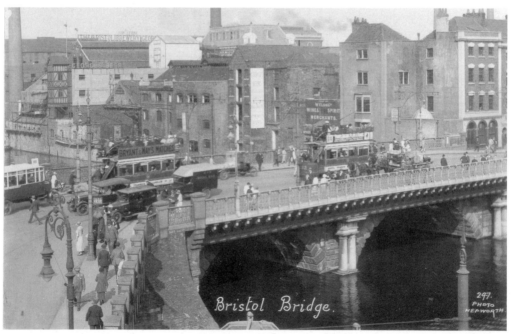

63. An interesting view of Bristol Bridge. Bristol derives its name from "Brigstow", meaning "settlement on the bridge". The original bridge was built in the 13th century, but the present bridge was built in 1768 and was designed by James Bridges. This view shows the original stone arches and pillars used to extend the width of the bridge in 1873. Across the river is George's Brewery, established in 1788.

64. St. Nicholas Church looking across Bristol Bridge from Victoria Street. The church was originally built in the 13th century, on part of the foundations of the old city wall. The crypt dates from 1370, and the clock one of the few public clocks with a minute hand.

65. Victoria Street, on a postcard postally used in 1910. This road was made across St. Thomas Street and Temple Street in 1871. The tram behind the tram pole on route from Knowle to Bristol Bridge. The Reynolds Hotel on the left became the offices of George's Brewery in 1919.

66. Temple Street. In front of the building on the left is Neptune's statue, in its third position. The statue was first erected in Temple Street in 1723, then moved to the end of the lane near Temple Church churchyard. The vicar of the church at that time had it moved to its position in this picture in 1872. The Shakespeare Inn is to the right of the advertisement hoarding.

67. Victoria Street. The George and Railway Hotel and just beyond the Grosvenor Hotel. Two rare freight wagons on the bridge, where the railway line ran through Bathhurst Basin to Wapping Wharf, c.1919.

68. Victoria Street by the bottom of Temple Meads Station incline, this is also referred to as Temple Gate, Brunel's Station, built in 1840, on the right. Tram no. 226 en route for Brislington. Postcard postally used in 1919.

69. The entrance to the Joint Station, the Great Western and Midland railway built in 1878. Note the imposing lamp standard in the middle of the road.

71. Redcliffe Street a flourishing thoroughfare c.1930, looking towards St. Mary Redcliffe Church. This graceful church dates from the 12th century. Elizabeth I rightly described the church as "The fairest, goodliest, and most famous parish church in England".

70. The old Shot Tower, Redcliffe Hill. Lead shot was invented by William Watts in 1782, by dropping lead with arsenic content 120 feet into a vat of cold water, the principle carried out to the present day. The original shot tower was removed for road widening in 1968.

72. Redcliffe Wharf looking towards Bristol Bridge. W.C.A. Mills, warehouse with a ship the "Sofia" of London moored by the quay. There are more warehouses further along, and on the opposite quay, ships unloading in Welsh Back. Postcard postally used in 1907.

73. A busy docks scene c.1880's, with a ship moored to the left from Penzance. Redcliffe Church and the terraced houses in Redcliffe Parade to the right.

74. A much later view of the docks from Prince Street swing bridge, constructed in 1879. John Robinson Oil and Coke Mills behind the dockside buildings on the right. Unloading is the "Juno" 1949-67, owned by the Bristol Steam Navigation Company.

75. A cargo ship being escorted by a tug after discharging her cargo at Princes Wharf. This view shows Bristol docks when it reached right up into the city centre. On the left one of the towers of Bristol Cathedral, and on the opposite corner Narrow Quay and the Bush Warehouse.

76. A ship belonging to the City Line, unloading at Prince's Wharf. The steamship moored alongside Narrow Quay is the S.S. Sarah of Cardiff and to the right, a three masted sailing ship unloading cargo, from Norway. This information is given on the back of this postcard written from Eastville.

77. The Floating Harbour at Hotwells, from the timber yards of Canada and Cumberland Wharf. Across the harbour moored on the Hotwells Road side, the "Daedelus", a Royal Navy Training Ship built at Sharpness in Gloucestershire in 1826. Postally used in 1906.

78. One of the Royal Navy training ships that continued to train boys for the navy "H.M.S. Flying Fox", moored at the same quay as the former training ship "Daedelus", adjoining Mardyke Ferry. The largest building on the hill in Clifton Wood, the Clifton Industrial School. To the right of the "Flying Fox" moored by the quay two of P & A Campbell's paddle steamers.

79. Queen Square from the roof of the Co-operative Wholesale building. The square covers five acres, with eight paths leading out from the centre. Into Prince Street, Rouch and Penny, electrical engineers, and further along several small shops mixed with warehouses, c.1910.

80. Queen Square built on land known as "The Marsh", and named after Queen Anne, who came with her husband, Prince George, to visit Bristol in 1702. The statue of William III designed by Rysbrack, was set up in 1736. This view c.1911 shows railings surrounding the statue, before the layout of the square was altered.

81. King Street looking towards the dock-side at Welsh Back, from the corner with Charlotte Street. The inn on the left "The Old Duke" still vibrates to the sounds of jazz! The poster on the side of the Llandoger Tavern advertises the "Little Drummer Boy" at the Theatre Royal (see illustration 84).

82. A fine view of the Llandoger Trow, the first house (on the nearest end) is the Llandoger Tavern. This row of houses was built in 1664. The origin of the name is thought to be from Llandogo a small town in the Wye Valley. The trow was a flat-bottomed boat which traded from Welsh Back up to the Wye Valley, regularly carrying a variety of goods to sell in Bristol.

83. King Street in the 1890's, the photo by Fred Little. Looking along King Street from Charlotte Street, the first house with a shell porch, next door to three gabled houses. The premises of the first house used by M. Fitzgerald dealer in marine stores, rope, rags and coal. Warehouses complete the picture. Today many in use as restaurants and pubs, with the cobbled road adding to the "olde worlde" atmosphere.

84. King Street, next to the two gabled houses is the Theatre Royal. This view shows its second frontage of 1903. The entrance when the theatre was built in 1766, had a two pillared porch. The theatre known as 'the old Theatre' is the oldest working theatre in the country. Adjoining is the Coopers Hall and St. Nicholas Almshouse.

85. Baldwin Street, the Fish, Game and Poultry market, owned by James Bigwood. When the market closed in the 1960's, it was owned by MacFisheries. The building is still in existence today, adjoining the steps to St. Nicholas Street. This view c.1908.

86. Baldwin Street built in 1881. This busy scene looking towards the tramway centre, a tram, two horse drawn carts, and the open cart nearest the pavement owned by the Bristol Corporation cleansing department.

THE PALACE THEATRE, BALDWIN STREET, BRISTOL.

87. The Palace Theatre opened in 1892, and was called "The Peoples Palace". A former theatre it later became the Gaumont Cinema, where an organ entertained the audience during the interval. It is now an entertainment centre. Postcard postally used in 1911.

88. Baldwin Street from the Tramway Centre. The tram travelling from Hotwells to Brislington. The horse and cart crossing the road belongs to Pickfords, the noted haulage firm, c.1914.

89. A view across the centre taken from the roof top of the Bristol Hippodrome. In the foreground the Dublin Shed adjoins the floating harbour, and in Broad Quay the premises with the two sun blinds down owned by Willways Garage.

90. Clare Street and Baldwin Street, this view c.1917. On the left below St. Stephens Church tower can be seen Clare Street Picture House, following to the right Christ Church, All Saints, and just visible the square tower of St. Mary-Le-Port Church and finally the spire of St. Nicholas church, earning Bristol the title of the 'City of Churches'.

INDEX